T5-AOI-317

"rolly-polly" balls of fur

By late April or early May, mama bear and her new babies are ready to explore the world around their winter home. By this time of their lives, the little bear cubs are small, "rolly-polly" balls of fur. The size of the bear family can be anywhere from just one cub to three. Sometimes when another mother bear is unable to take care of her cub, the little bear will be cared for by a mama bear with her own cubs. When this happens the mama bear has a very busy spring taking care of as many as four cubs.

Springtime is sort of a hard time for the bear family. There isn't a lot of food around and for the first few weeks the bears must depend on the fat that they have stored up through the winter. Nights are still cool at this time of year and the family doesn't move very far during the daylight hours.

happy sounds...

Mama bear is one of the very best moms at taking care of her babies. Everything that happens to the bear family in the early weeks out of the den is a very important lesson. The little bears have plenty of time to play and search for food but a large part of the time is spent resting. Many of the rest periods are times when the cubs are able to nurse from the mother bear. Nursing is necessary for the baby bears so that they can keep growing stronger from the mother's milk. These times of resting and nursing are the best times in the little bears' day. If there are two or three cubs, each bear finds a special spot under Mom's big arms. The sounds that are made by the babies as they nurse are very happy sounds. It is something like a purr, a humm, and a buzz, all at the same time. The mother bear watches the babies with much love and soon all may fall asleep for a little while.

A purr,

a humm, and a buzz,

all at the same time

Nap Time...

Some little bears are much like some little boys and girls. When the rest of the family wants to sleep, one little bear may want to play. Mama bear is very patient with the little playful cub until she sees that he may be disturbing the other cubs. When this happens, Mom may just put her big paw on top of the little restless cub so that he knows that it is nap time. This shows the little bear that Mom knows best and the feel of Mom's loving paw next to him helps him to drop off into a good sleep.

The rule with baby bears... do whatever Mom does

If there is one special thing that bears are very good at, it must be climbing. Some folks say that a bear can climb a tree faster than a person can fall out of one. This must be true because very soon after leaving the den the little bears get to try their luck at climbing. Usually Mom finds a tree with some real tasty leaves just starting to open up. After sniffing around the bottom the mother bear gives off a huff and up the tree she goes. The best leaves are at the top so up and up she climbs. The rule with baby bears is to do whatever Mom does first, so up they go. Even though their little claws are still small, they are very sharp and the cubs hold tightly to the bark of the tree. Sometimes the cubs get in a hurry and forget to hold on tight and they bounce down the tree or at least slide down a little ways. This doesn't hurt a baby bear and he just gets right up and goes back up the tree until he is as high as Mom.

After all

It would have been a lot easier if Mom could have picked out a low branch and pulled it down for the little cubs to eat on. The truth is that Mom knows that these little bears will be big bears in a couple of years and they must learn the rules of nature very early if they are to become strong and healthy bears themselves. After all, it is safer up in the top of the tree and a young, tender leaf in the top of the tree surely gets more sunshine and probably tastes lots better.

it is safer up in the top of the tree

When he finds just the right limb

After long mornings of climbing trees and digging into old fallen logs in the forest, it usually is resting time again during the warmer parts of the afternoon. Bears make their beds close to trees in case that there is danger and the cubs should need to climb to safety. Sometimes the baby bears decide to take their nap right up in the tree. When a baby bear finds just the right limb, he just lets his little legs hang right down while he snoozes away the afternoon. Even baby bears are very good at keeping their balance so that they don't fall from their resting spot.

...he snoozes away the afternoon

There are lots of "forest friends"

In this brand new world of the baby bear there are lots of "forest friends" to get acquainted with. Many of these fellows that the little bear meets in the forest are also youngsters. This calls for some real fun while each little animal tries to find out what the other is up to. In case the little cub bumps into a rabbit, there is almost always a short chase which the little bear loses. If Mr. Skunk should happen to be shuffling around the woods when the little bear comes to play, it could get pretty smelly for a while. Raccoons are cousins of the black bear so each "critter" just seems content to sniff around the other and go on their merry way. A woodchuck or groundhog, as it is cleverly called, is never far from his hole in case a nosy little bear decides to play too rough. Many times as the bear family wanders through the forest a deer will become surprised by the visit and scamper about the woods until it realizes that this friendly bear family means no harm. It sure is hard to make friends with a turtle, though. No matter how gently the little bear flips the turtle over and over, Mr. Turtle is always content to spend extra time inside his shell until the little bear goes away.

As the days get longer and summer arrives, the forest is covered with many tender plants and berries for the baby bears to eat. The bears start to travel further from homebase to find their favorite foods. The berry patches are very tempting places to spend the mornings and evenings. Bears often visit berry patches that are very near to farms or ranches. The little bears are always very near to Mom when people smells are in the air. Even though the cubs are young, they can already run fast and climb high if they are frightened.

Things can get pretty crowded...

The mother bear seems to have many ways to talk to her babies. Sometimes a "huff" or a stomp on the ground tells the little bears to head for the nearest tree while Mom checks the wind for unusual smells. If mama bear is frightened, she may run toward the cubs so that they know to be extra quick in climbing a tree. If all the baby bears try to climb the tree at the same time, things can get pretty crowded and someone is going to have to wait.

someone

is going to

have to wait

Climbing a tree for safety or just for fun

If a little bear is climbing a tree for safety or just for fun, it is always a challenge to see who can get high in the tree first. Sometimes the cubs make whining sounds when their brother or sister will not let them get higher up in the tree. When this happens, the bear cub just sits in the saddle of the tree while the little bear above him kicks tree bark down on him. All the time the baby bears are learning important lessons and growing stronger.

...shyly he obeys her command...

The bear family continues to enjoy the tasty foods of the forest all through the summer until the fall when the acorns fall from the oak trees. The mother bear lets the cubs explore on their own as long as they do not get too far away. If Mom should look for a cub and he is not there, she will go after him and scold him for wandering away from the others. The little bear seems to understand that Mom is doing what is best for him and shyly he obeys her command to stay with the other cubs.

to stay with the other cubs

The bears are our friends

Since we love to walk through the forest, now we know more about the baby bears that live there. The bears are our friends and when bears live in the forest we know that the forest is healthy. If we see a baby bear in a tree, we don't need to be afraid. If we leave the little bear to eat and play, then we have helped to keep Nature safe and undisturbed. When we can share the forest with the bear we have become friends with the wilderness and many people for many years will be able to enjoy the world of baby bears.

Save a Place for Bears